To my mother Esmat, who inspire me to write,

"Raising knowledgeable kids is like giving them wings to fly high and explore the world with confidence and curiosity."

CHAPTER 1: THE MAGICAL SEED

Once upon a time, there was a little girl named Lily who lived with her mom. Lily loved spending time with her grandfather, who was a wise old man with a long white beard. One day, her grandfather gave her a special gift before he passed away. It was a small seed that sparkled in the sunlight.

"Lily, this is a magical seed," her grandfather said with a twinkle in his eye. "Plant it and take care of it, and one day it will give you a fruit that will allow you to fly and travel the world."

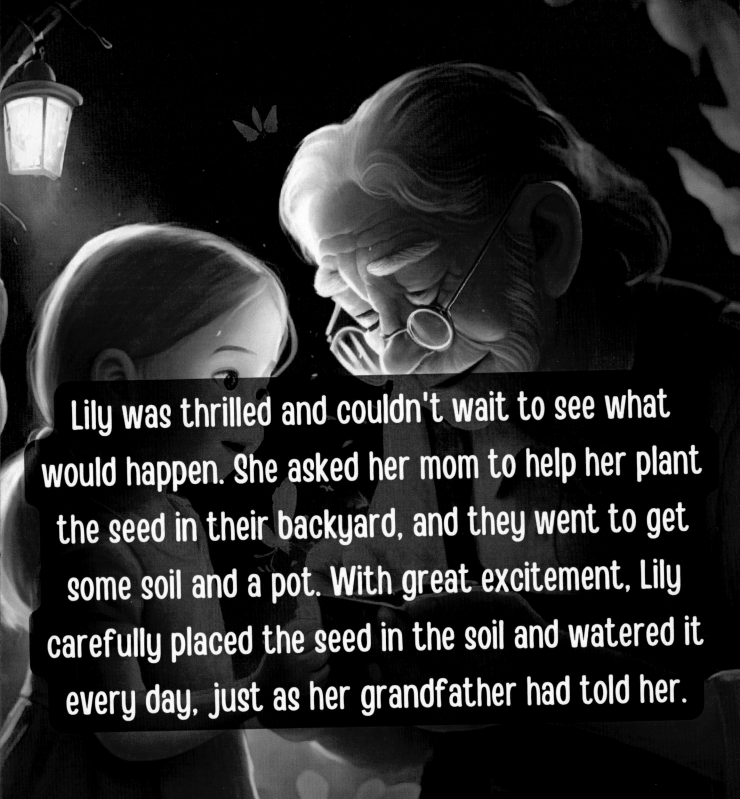

Lily was thrilled and couldn't wait to see what would happen. She asked her mom to help her plant the seed in their backyard, and they went to get some soil and a pot. With great excitement, Lily carefully placed the seed in the soil and watered it every day, just as her grandfather had told her.

CHAPTER 2: CARING FOR THE PLANT

Months went by, and Lily watched the plant grow taller and taller. She took great care of it, making sure it had enough sunlight and water. She even sang to it, believing that her sweet voice would help it grow faster. Lily was patient and persistent, and soon the plant started to have beautiful blossoms.

Lily's mom was proud of her daughter's dedication and hard work. She encouraged Lily to keep taking care of the plant, reminding her of the special fruit that would come one day. Lily was determined to see the fruit and eagerly waited for it to appear.

CHAPTER 3: THE RED APPLE

One day, as Lily was checking her plant, she noticed something extraordinary. There was a fruit growing on it, and it looked like a red apple! Lily's eyes widened with excitement, and she could hardly contain her joy. She had been dreaming of this moment for so long.

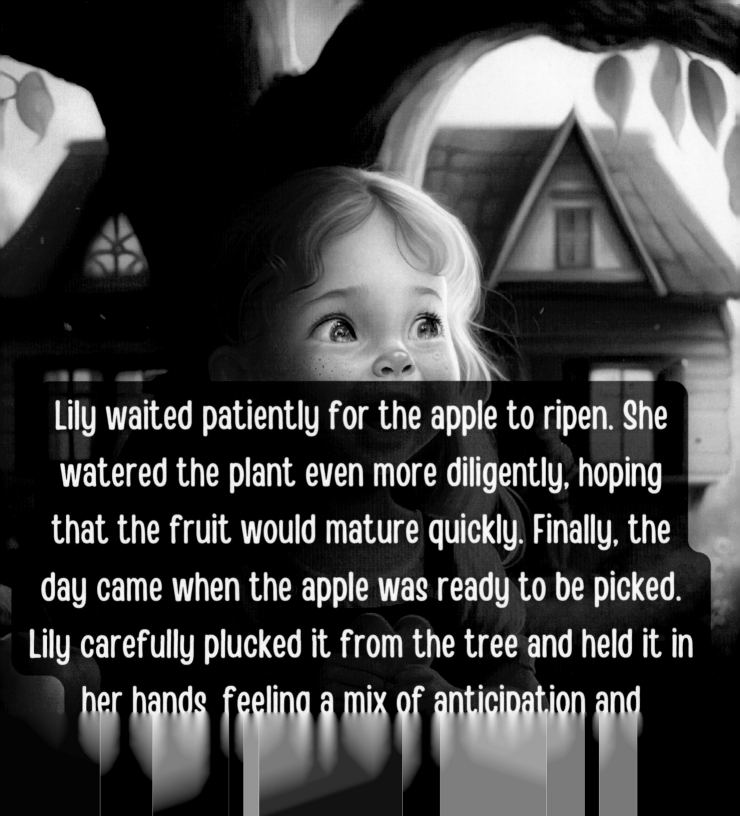

Lily waited patiently for the apple to ripen. She watered the plant even more diligently, hoping that the fruit would mature quickly. Finally, the day came when the apple was ready to be picked. Lily carefully plucked it from the tree and held it in her hands, feeling a mix of anticipation and

CHAPTER 4: DISAPPOINTMENT

Lily was excited to eat the apple, she thought it would make her fly and go on adventures around the world. She took a big bite of the apple, but sadly, nothing magical happened. She couldn't fly and was still in her backyard....

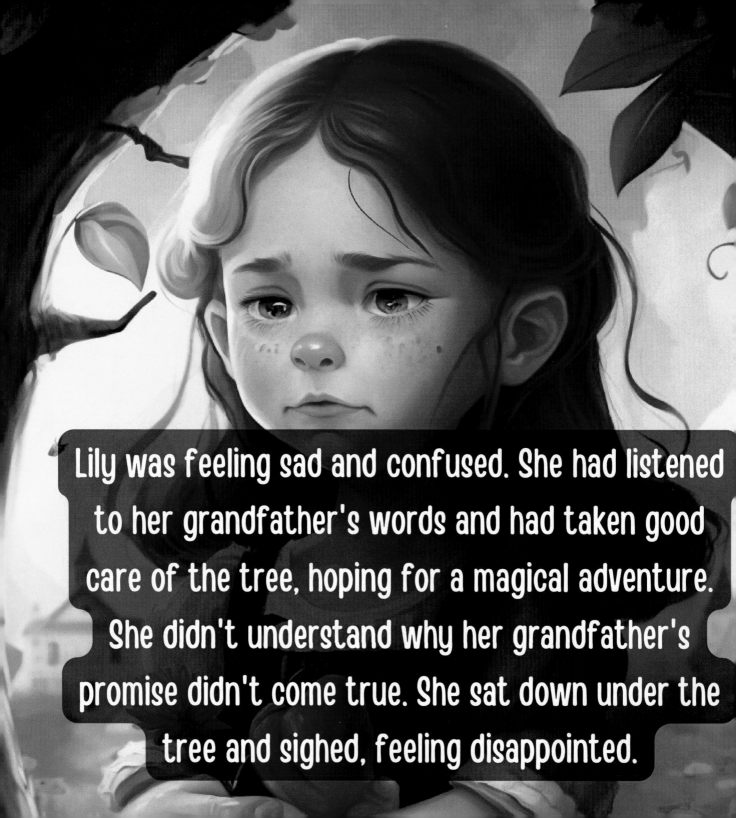

Lily was feeling sad and confused. She had listened to her grandfather's words and had taken good care of the tree, hoping for a magical adventure. She didn't understand why her grandfather's promise didn't come true. She sat down under the tree and sighed, feeling disappointed.

CHAPTER 5: A LESSON FROM MOM

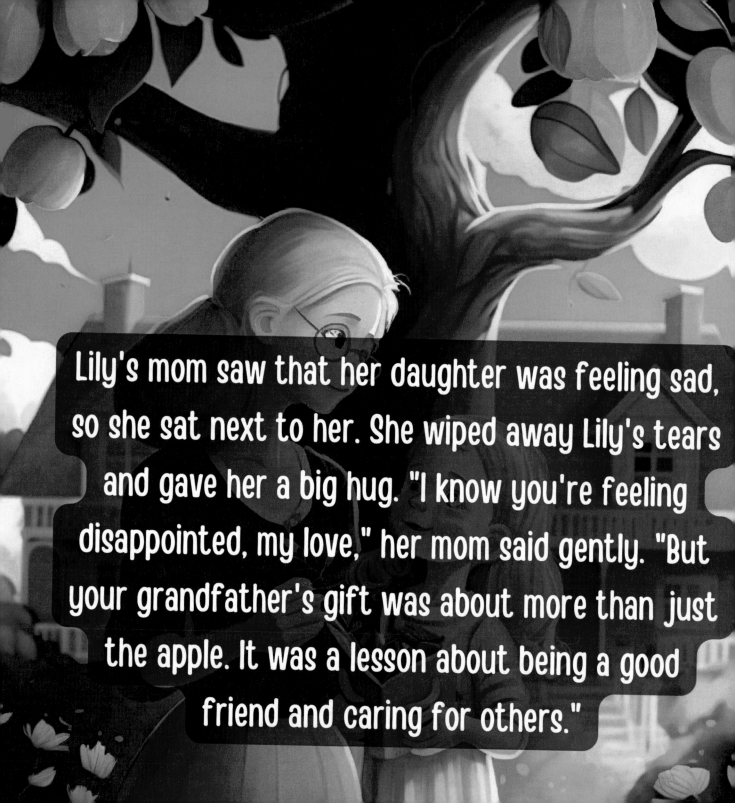

Lily's mom saw that her daughter was feeling sad, so she sat next to her. She wiped away Lily's tears and gave her a big hug. "I know you're feeling disappointed, my love," her mom said gently. "But your grandfather's gift was about more than just the apple. It was a lesson about being a good friend and caring for others."

Lily looked up at her mom, curious. Her mom continued, "You see, by taking care of the plant every day, you have developed a special bond with it. You have a friend now, and that's something truly magical."

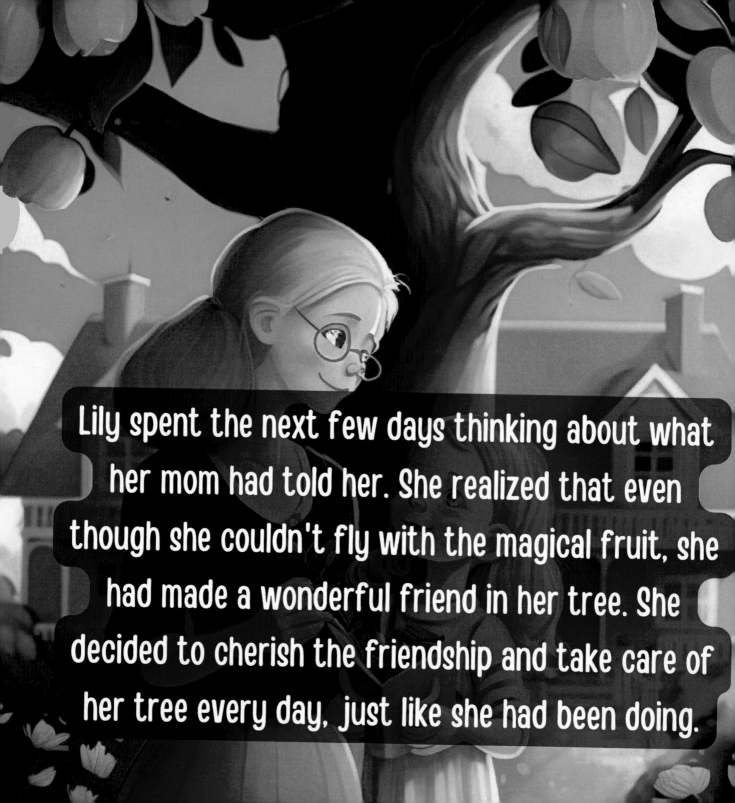

Lily spent the next few days thinking about what her mom had told her. She realized that even though she couldn't fly with the magical fruit, she had made a wonderful friend in her tree. She decided to cherish the friendship and take care of her tree every day, just like she had been doing.

CHAPTER 6: LILI'S FRIENDS

One day, while Lily was watering her tree, her friends Sally and Anna came over to visit. They were amazed by the beautiful tree and the magical fruit. Lily told them the whole story about her grandfather and how she had learned the importance of friendship from her tree.

Sally and Anna were excited to be a part of the magical adventure. They offered to help Lily take care of the tree and waited eagerly for the fruit to ripen. They spent their afternoons playing near the tree and imagining all the places they could visit with the magical fruit.

Finally, the day arrived when the fruit turned ripe and red. Lily, Sally, and Anna couldn't contain their excitement. They plucked the fruit from the tree and held it in their hands. They looked at each other with big smiles on their faces, ready to embark on their grand adventure.

CHAPTER 7: ALWAYS LOVING AND CARING FRIENDS

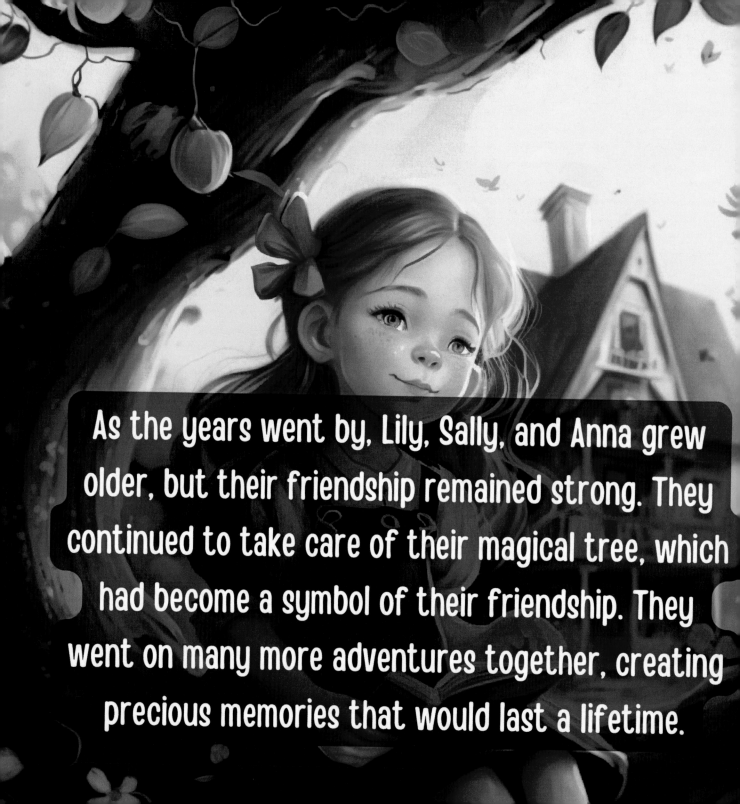

As the years went by, Lily, Sally, and Anna grew older, but their friendship remained strong. They continued to take care of their magical tree, which had become a symbol of their friendship. They went on many more adventures together, creating precious memories that would last a lifetime.

Lily was sad that the fruit from her magic tree didn't make her fly like her grandpa promised. But then she remembered something important. Her grandpa wanted her to learn that taking care of her tree every day was like taking care of a good friend. Lily realized that even though she didn't get to fly, she had something special to be grateful for. She learned that friendships are like planting a seed and taking care of it. The more you take care of it, the stronger and more fun it gets.

Lily was happy to have her tree and all the good friends in her life, and she knew that taking care of them was the real magic that made life great. She smiled and said, "Thank you, grandpa, for teaching me such an important lesson."